Nicaragua

Nicaragua

BY WIL MARA

Enchantment of the World™
Second Series

CHILDREN'S PRESS®
An Imprint of Scholastic Inc.

Frontispiece: **Concepción Volcano**

Consultant: Daniel Chávez, Assistant Professor, Department of Languages, Literatures, and Cultures, University of New Hampshire, Durham, New Hampshire
Please note: All statistics are as up-to-date as possible at the time of publication.

Book production by The Design Lab

Library of Congress Cataloging-in-Publication Data
Names: Mara, Wil, author.
Title: Nicaragua / by Wil Mara.
Description: New York : Children's Press, [2016] | Series: Enchantment of the world
  | Includes bibliographical references and index.
Identifiers: LCCN 2016025113 | ISBN 9780531220900 (library binding)
Subjects: LCSH: Nicaragua—Juvenile literature.
Classification: LCC F1523.2 .M35 2016 | DDC 972.85—dc23
LC record available at https://lccn.loc.gov/2016025113

1 2 3 4 5 6 7 8 9 10 R 26 25 24 23 22 21 20 19 18 17

Girl selling cashews

Contents

Left to right: **Little Corn Island, León church, scarlet macaw, El Güegüense performance, traditional clothing**

CHAPTER 1

Land of Eternal Hope

ALEJANDRO AND MARÍA ARE PLAYING IN THE backyard of their home on the outskirts of Managua, the capital of the Central American nation of Nicaragua. It's getting close to dinnertime, and they know their mother will be calling them inside soon. Alejandro is throwing a ball against the wall of the house and catching it in his baseball mitt when it comes back. Sometimes it bounces high in the air, and other times it skips along the ground. He does this for hours after school most days. Alejandro gets good grades in school, but his big dream is to play for Nicaragua's national baseball team one day. The team's players are considered heroes in Nicaragua, and some of them get to go to the United States and play professional baseball there. This makes them rich and famous, which sounds great to Alejandro.

Opposite: **Baseball is the most popular sport in Nicaragua.**

He looks over at his sister, who is sitting under a guava tree reading a book. Her dream is to become a teacher. She is very smart, Alejandro knows, and he wants to see her succeed more than anything. Their mother was a good student, too, but she did not get the education she needed to reach her own dreams. She and Alejandro's father grew up in a time when Nicaragua was going through a lot of conflict. The government was unstable, and food and water weren't always available. Alejandro's

parents tell horrible stories about soldiers coming to their homes at night and stealing their things. One of Alejandro's uncles was even killed while fighting for a group called the Sandinistas. Alejandro and his sister never got to meet him, but their mother tells wonderful stories about him.

Their parents talk all the time about wanting Alejandro and María to have a better life than they did. They want them to have their own homes, their own careers, and maybe get married and have children. "But above all else, we want the two of you to be happy," they say. Alejandro wonders if this is even

Managua lies on the shores of Lake Managua. The city has been Nicaragua's capital since 1852.

possible. He and María have friends at school who come from very poor families that barely have enough to eat.

Alejandro's father earns good money working in a clothing factory, so food isn't a problem for his family. They grow fruits, vegetables, and herbs in their backyard, too. But Alejandro still has this nagging feeling that it could all disappear at any moment. His parents tell him the country is stronger than it has been in a long time, and that things are getting better. They just wish it would get better faster. Alejandro wishes that, too.

More than eighty thousand people work in Nicaragua's textile factories.

Alejandro throws the ball against the house a few more times. It doesn't seem to bother María in the least. She is lost in that book of hers. He has always been impressed by how well she can concentrate. He knows she is trying her best with her schoolwork. And their mother is trying her best to take care of them. And their father works hard at his job. Alejandro has every intention of doing his best as well—at his studies, at his baseball practice, at everything. But will it be enough in a place that has seen such hard times? Will it be enough in Nicaragua, a nation that sometimes seems to be teetering between unmatched success and continued failure?

He hopes so.

Boys play baseball on the beach by Lake Nicaragua.

CHAPTER 2

Land of Lakes and Volcanoes

NICARAGUA IS ONE OF SEVEN COUNTRIES IN THE southernmost section of the North American continent, an area known as Central America. Together, these seven nations form a narrow link between Mexico and South America. Nicaragua's closest neighbors are Honduras to the north and Costa Rica to the south. To the west is the Pacific Ocean, and to the east is the Caribbean Sea.

Nicaragua and its neighbors lie in the tropics. This is the area near the equator, an imaginary line around the globe halfway between the North and the South Poles. Places in the tropics are warm year-round. Most are also quite humid, frequently receiving heavy rainfall.

Opposite: **Palm trees line the beaches in the Corn Islands, Nicaraguan islands in the Caribbean Sea.**

Nicaragua's Geographic Features

Area: 50,336 square miles (130,370 sq km)

Highest Point: Mogotón Peak, at 6,909 feet (2,106 m)

Lowest Point: Sea level along the coasts

Largest Lake: Lake Nicaragua, 3,149 square miles (8,157 sq km)

Longest River: Coco, 485 miles (780 km)

Average High Temperature: In Managua, 88°F (31°C) in January, 88°F (31°C) in July

Average Low Temperature: In Managua, 69°F (20°C) in January, 73°F (23°C) in July

Average Annual Precipitation: Varies from 75 inches (190 cm) in the west to up to 250 inches (635 cm) in the east

Nicaragua has an area of about 50,336 square miles (130,370 square kilometers). This makes it fairly modest in size by American standards—it is slightly larger than the U.S. state of Mississippi—but large in comparison to its neighboring countries. In fact, it is the largest nation in Central America.

From East to West

Nicaragua can be divided into three main sections—the Caribbean lowlands that lie near the ocean in the east, the highlands in the country's central region, and the Pacific Lowlands in the west.

Clouds hang low amid the forests in the steep mountains near Matagalpa, in central Nicaragua.

Central Nicaragua is covered in mountains.

The Caribbean lowland makes up about half of Nicaragua's area. The flat land here is filled with sparse woodland savannas and dense rain forests. Along the coast, there are many marshes and mangrove swamps. The soil in the region is not fertile, so there is little agriculture. This is the hottest and most humid part of the country. The Caribbean lowland is less densely populated than the rest of the country, accounting for about 10 percent of the nation's population. Its major cities include Puerto Cabezas in the north and Bluefields in the south. Other smaller cities dot the region.

Nicaragua's Central Highlands are marked by extensive mountain ranges separated by forested valleys. The tallest mountains are in the north. The Entre Ríos range, along the Honduran border, includes the nation's highest point, Mogotón Peak, which reaches 6,909 feet (2,106 m) above sea level. The Isabella and Dariense ranges are in north-central Nicaragua, while the Amerrisque range runs all the way from Costa Rica through Nicaragua to western Honduras. Many people consider the Amerrisque Mountains the dividing line between Nicaragua's eastern and western halves.

The climate in the Central Highlands is much cooler and less humid than in the lowlands. As such, Nicaraguans have farmed the region for centuries. In particular, the western side of many mountains, protected from winds that roll in from the east, have been fertile ground for farmers to grow grains, fruits, vegetables, and coffee.

A boy tends cabbage plants in the Central Highlands.

Nicaraguans watch hot ash and lava erupt from Momotombo. The volcano lies near the city of León.

The Pacific Lowlands are where most of Nicaragua's farming, commerce, industry, and tourism take place. The soil is fertile, the climate is pleasant, and much of the land is flat. There are many rivers and lakes there. Most Nicaraguans live in the Pacific Lowlands.

This region is also the site of Nicaragua's volcanoes. There are about twenty of them, and most are active. Some haven't erupted for thousands of years, but others have rumbled in recent times. Momotombo, for example, erupted for the first time in 110 years in 2015, sending hot rock and ash into the air.

For most of history, ships traveling from the Atlantic Ocean to the Pacific had to sail all the way around Cape Horn at the southern tip of South America. The trip could take months. In 1848, gold was discovered in California. Many people in the eastern United States were in a hurry to get to California in the hopes of making a fortune. Rather than traveling all the way around Cape Horn, many of them traveled up the San Juan River and across Lake Nicaragua. From there, it was just a short journey to the Pacific where they could sail north to California. The route across Nicaragua was one of the quickest ways between the oceans until the Panama Canal opened in 1914, giving ships a water route across the narrow nation of Panama.

Rivers and Lakes

Nicaragua is a land of many rivers and lakes. Lake Nicaragua, in the southwest of the country, is the nation's largest lake and the second-largest in all of Latin America, trailing only Lake Maracaibo in Venezuela. It spreads across 3,149 square miles (8,157 sq km), making it larger than the U.S. state of Delaware. Hundreds of islands rise above the waters in Lake Nicaragua. The largest, Ometepe, is made from two extinct volcanoes. Ometepe is home to about thirty thousand people. Other major islands in the lake include Zapatera and the Solentiname Islands.

One of the nation's most storied rivers is the San Juan, which runs out of Lake Nicaragua in the east. It forms much of the border between Nicaragua and Costa Rica and then empties into the Caribbean. It has been used for transport for centuries.

Nicaragua's longest river is the Coco River, which stretches 485 miles (780 km), starting in Honduras and flowing into Nicaragua in the northeast. Another major river, Tipitapa, connects Lake Nicaragua with another large lake, Lake Managua, to the northwest.

Islands

Nicaragua has about twenty major islands off its coast, along with many other smaller islands. These islands, renowned for their beauty, attract many tourists. Most popular are Big Corn Island and Little Corn Island, located in the Caribbean Sea off Nicaragua's northeastern coast. Though they are small—the larger one covers just 3.9 square miles (10 sq km)—they feature many hotels, restaurants, and shops in addition to lovely beaches.

The Corn Islands attract scuba divers, snorkelers, and many other tourists.

A Look at Nicaragua's Cities

Managua, the capital city of Nicaragua, is the nation's largest city, with about a million residents, one-sixth of Nicaragua's total population. Other Nicaraguan cities, while not as large, are also significant.

León (below), located near the northwestern coast, is Nicaragua's second-largest city. It has a population of about 145,000, with another several hundred thousand people living nearby. León was Nicaragua's capital until Managua was given that title in the mid-1800s. Many Spanish colonial buildings still stand in the city, including the Cathedral of León, one of the largest churches in Central America. León is also an important center of education, agriculture, and industry.

Northwest of Lake Nicaragua is the city of Masaya. It has an estimated population of about 130,000, making it Nicaragua's third-largest city. It is a bustling center of business, acting as a hub for both agricultural and industrial production. In Masaya are many retail markets selling everything from handcrafts and clothing to fruits, vegetables, and meats.

Fourth in size is Tipitapa, with a population of about 127,000. It is located in the narrow area between Lake Nicaragua and Lake Managua. The city dates to the late 1700s, and it features many colonial-era buildings.

Cars and a motorcycle drive down a flooded street in Managua following heavy rains. In Managua, it rains an average of 122 days per year.

Climate

Nicaragua's climate is warm year-round. It is generally cooler in the highlands than in the lowlands, but even in the mountains it is rare for temperatures to drop below 60 degrees Fahrenheit (16 degrees Celsius) at night. There is little in the way of temperature variation overall, with an average range of between 70°F and 80°F (21°C and 27°C). The warmest time of the year is from late April to early May, and the coolest months are December and January.

Much more significant is the variation in how much rain falls. In Nicaragua, the year can be split into two seasons—the rainy season and the dry season. On the Caribbean side of the country, the rainy season lasts from June to February, while on the Pacific side, it is a couple months shorter, lasting from about May to November. At the height of the rainy season, it pours every afternoon. At the beginning and end of the rainy season, the rain is gentler. During the dry season, there is virtually no rain at all.

In total, the Caribbean side of the country gets much more rain than the Pacific side. The Pacific side averages about 75 inches (190 centimeters) of rain per year, while the Caribbean side can get up to 250 inches (635 cm). The Caribbean coast is also struck by more severe storms than the Pacific region, with tropical storms and hurricanes sometimes barreling across the landscape. When these hit, flooding is inevitable. The floodwaters destroy homes and crops, forcing Nicaraguans to find shelter elsewhere.

Hurricane Mitch

One of the most severe storms to hit the region in recent times was Hurricane Mitch, which pounded Nicaragua and neighboring nations in late October and early November of 1998. At the peak of its power, Mitch had a sustained wind speed of 180 miles per hour (290 kph). It dumped more than 4 feet (120 cm) of rain in some parts of Nicaragua. In Nicaragua alone, it made almost three-fourths of the roadways unusable, damaged or destroyed nearly fifty thousand homes, forced more than 350,000 people from their homes, and caused nearly four thousand deaths—second only to Honduras, which lost more than fourteen thousand people. The overall devastation was even worse in neighboring Honduras. In total, the storm killed more than nineteen thousand people.

Land of Lakes and Volcanoes **25**

CHAPTER 3

Wild Things

NICARAGUA'S WARM, TROPICAL ENVIRONMENT IS also very wet, with plenty of rain and rivers. Much of the land is covered in forest, while some lowland areas are swampy. With so much warmth and available water, Nicaragua is host to literally thousands of plant and animal species. Nearly everything grows well here. As a result of the diversity of wildlife and the abundance of fruits and flowers, Nicaragua's environment is vivid and colorful.

Mammals

Nicaragua is home to a tremendous variety of mammals, including lemurs, monkeys, rabbits, manatees, armadillos, anteaters, mice, rats, whales, bats, and wild dogs and cats. Among the most common is the mantled howler monkey, which is

Opposite: **The mantled howler monkey, the largest monkey in Nicaragua, spends most of its time in the trees. It is called a howler because the males' low calls can carry for more than 2 miles (3 km).**

Ocelots are bigger than a house cat but smaller than a leopard. They live throughout most of Latin America, as well as in the U.S. states of Texas and Arizona.

found throughout the country. It spends most of its time in trees, where it looks for the soft, young leaves that make up the bulk of its diet. Its tail acts very much like a fifth hand, curling around branches so it can swing about freely.

Another impressive Nicaraguan mammal is the ocelot. The ocelot looks like a miniature leopard and is sometimes called the dwarf leopard. Adults reach a length of about 35 inches (89 cm), not including the tail, and weigh 20 to 35 pounds (9 to 16 kilograms), about the same as a medium-sized dog. The ocelot is a solitary creature, prowling for food during the night and frequently resting in trees during the day. It is a carnivore, or meat eater, dining on just about anything it can hunt and kill, such as other mammals, birds, reptiles, and fish.

Reptiles and Amphibians

Reptiles and amphibians are often secretive creatures, and they frequently go overlooked and unseen. Hikers have walked past countless species without even realizing it. Many shelter under rocks, burrow beneath rotting trees, slither down holes in the ground, or rest on the bottoms of lakes and rivers, well away from people. Reptiles and amphibians are cold-blooded, meaning they cannot regulate their body temperature. Their body temperature goes up when they are in warm places and down when they are in cool places. As such, they do not tolerate cold weather well and thrive in tropical locales like Nicaragua.

The red-eyed tree frog is one of dozens of kinds of frogs that live in Nicaragua. The pads of its orange feet are sticky, and the frog often spends its days attached to the bottom of a leaf, asleep.

Male Hercules beetles can be easily identified by the hornlike structures on the tops of their heads. These are often used to fight other males over a mate.

Bugs and More

Thousands of types of bugs and other creepy-crawly creatures live in Nicaragua. Spiders, scorpions, beetles, ants, flies, millipedes, and centipedes are all found there. Most are harmless, but some kinds of spiders and scorpions do bite or sting.

One of the most remarkable insects in Nicaragua is the Hercules beetle. Most beetles are small enough to rest comfortably on a coin, but not the Hercules beetle. Adults can reach over half a foot (15 cm) in length, making them longer than many human hands! If that isn't creepy enough, the Hercules beetle's bizarre appearance is like something out of science fiction. It has six spindly legs extending from an oval, shell-covered body and a head that—at least on the males—

has a vertical pair of hornlike pincers. It can give quite a pinch when irritated. The Hercules beetle feeds primarily on fruit that has fallen to the forest floor, but when fruits aren't available, it will eat whatever other decaying plant matter is nearby, including rotted trees.

Sea Life

More than a hundred species of freshwater fish live in Nicaragua, and many more are found in the ocean nearby. The lakes are filled with a wide variety of fish, including tarpon, sawfish, and gaspar. Nicaragua is also home to a broad variety of shrimp, crabs, clams, and lobsters.

French grunt (yellow) and other fish swim near Big Corn Island. The island is encircled by a coral reef, which provides a home for a wide variety of sea life.

Fish Troubles

In Nicaragua, many fish species are in decline because of the fishing industry. Fishing is not just a sport but a means of survival in Nicaragua, as many people rely on catching fish as part of their staple diet. Similarly, local fishers sustain themselves on what they can catch and then sell either to markets or directly to consumers. Two people with a net can remove literally thousands of fish from lakes and rivers, significantly depleting those populations. Sport fishing is also popular, as fishers head just off the coast to catch marlin, tuna, sailfish, and more.

Some people also catch fish to sell in the pet trade. For example, many kinds of cichlids, which are common in Lake Nicaragua and elsewhere, are in great demand for aquariums.

The most surprising creature found there is the bull shark, an ocean shark that can survive in the fresh water of Lake Nicaragua. It travels between the lake and ocean via the San Juan River.

Large, slow-moving mammals called manatees also live in the San Juan. Manatees are endangered, but a sanctuary has been established in the river to give them a place safe from boats and hunters.

Plant Life

Due to the favorable climate, Nicaragua is home to hundreds of different tree species. Many are hardy, and can grow everywhere from the cool and rugged mountain regions to the sandy shores of the nation's coastlines. The forests are filled with everything from pine, cedar, and mahogany to very hard woods such as quebracho and guaiacum.

Mangrove trees grow along the Caribbean coast. These trees grow in salt water, and their tangle of roots below the water's surface creates a safe home for young fish and other sea life. Mangrove swamps also help protect the land from powerful, destructive ocean waves.

Fruit trees abound in Nicaragua. Without realizing it, you

Hikers make their way through a rain forest in southern Nicaragua. The forest is filled with ancient trees and dense underbrush.

How Sweet

The fruit of the guaba tree is the source of one of the most delightful treats in all of Nicaragua. The tree itself grows to a height of about 60 feet (18 meters). It has a mushroom-like appearance in that its relatively narrow trunk leads up to a broad canopy. From a distance, it seems unremarkable compared to most other trees. Up close, however, people can see that hanging from the branches are long, tubular fruits that look like giant peapods. They are, in fact, related to beans and lentils. When the pods are cut open they reveal a line of large seeds covered in a white layer of what feels like velvet. This part of the fruit is wonderfully sweet and can be eaten on the spot. Many Nicaraguan children love guaba, and it is often called the ice cream bean.

may have enjoyed lemons, limes, oranges, bananas, melons, coconuts, and pineapples that were grown on a Nicaraguan farm. Many other kinds of less common fruit trees such as grosella, guaba, jocote, and guanabana also grow in Nicaragua.

Breadfruit, another fruit that is rare in the United States, is popular in many places in Nicaragua. In particular, it grows in abundance along the Caribbean coast. The tree reaches a height of about 46 feet (14 m). When mature, the fruit itself can range from the size of a baseball to a large cantaloupe. Breadfruit is bright green with a knobby outer texture. It is rich in vitamins and can be prepared any number of ways, including frying and baking. It gets its name, in fact, from what it looks like after baking, when it has both the texture and appearance of bread.

National Flower

The sacuanjoche is Nicaragua's national flower. The variety most celebrated in the country has five long, white petals with a gentle spray of vivid yellow toward the center of the star. The flower appears on a cone-shaped tree that is remarkably hardy and grows throughout Nicaragua and in other tropical regions around the world. In Nicaragua, the tree begins to bloom in May and produces a sweet scent.

As with many tropical places, Nicaragua is host to an explosive array of colorful plants and flowers. Everything from hardy cacti to delicate hibiscuses thrive there. Orchids, lilies, mosses, and ferns fill the forest.

Some breadfruit grows up to 1 foot (30 cm) long. Inside is a simple white substance that tastes something like a potato.

CHAPTER 4

Years Past

EXPERTS BELIEVE THAT THE EARLIEST PEOPLE TO settle in the region known today as Nicaragua came both from the north (what are now Mexico and Guatemala) and the south (what are now Colombia and Panama) some time around the sixth century BCE. Those from the north were likely associated with the Aztec and Mayan civilizations. They tended to settle in the central and western areas. Most of the indigenous, or native, people from this region spoke some form of Pipil, a language similar to that spoken by the Aztecs. People migrating from the south ended up along the eastern coast in the Caribbean Lowlands and used a language similar to Chibcha, which is spoken in Colombia.

In time, three distinct groups formed in what is now Nicaragua, each with its own culture—the Chontal, the Chorotega, and the Nicarao. The Nicarao lived along the Pacific coast. In time, their name would give the country its name.

Opposite: **Ancient people carved large statues on islands in Lake Nicaragua roughly a thousand years ago.**

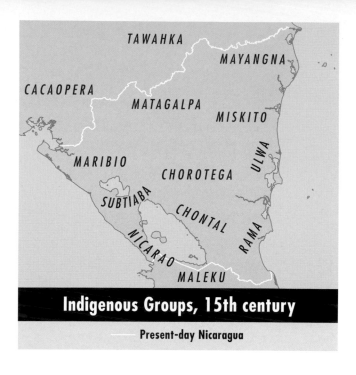

Indigenous Groups, 15th century

Present-day Nicaragua

Spain Takes Over

Starting in the late 1400s, the nation of Spain made a vigorous effort to expand its influence around the world. People from Spain and other European nations began exploring parts of the Western Hemisphere. They hoped to conquer the lands and take the natural resources they found there. The Spaniards who traveled to the Americas also wanted to spread the Roman Catholic religion to the indigenous people. They believed the people they encountered in the Western Hemisphere were inferior and hoped to "civilize" them.

The Spaniards who led these missions to the Americas were called conquistadores. One of the best-known conquistadores is Christopher Columbus, an Italian working for Spain. He made four journeys to the Americas starting in 1492. It was during his final voyage, in 1502, that he found and explored the eastern coastline of what is now Nicaragua. Columbus and his crew remained in the area for about two months. News of Columbus's discoveries in the Western Hemisphere spread quickly back home in Europe, and it wasn't long before Spanish leaders dispatched other conquistadores to the region. In 1519, a Spaniard named Hernán Cortés led a campaign to Mexico. Shrewd and ruthless, Cortés determined that the heart of the region was controlled by the Aztecs, so

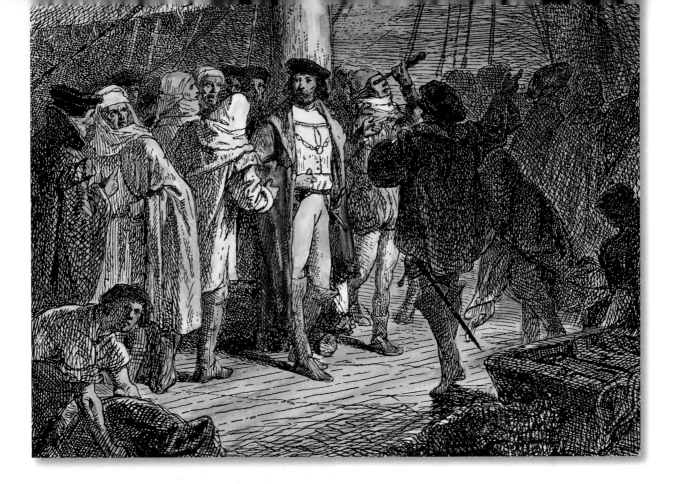

he allied himself with smaller groups who resented Aztec rule. Over time, he replaced Aztec rule with his own. By 1521, he was firmly in control of the Aztec lands. Now that the Spanish had a solid foothold in the Americas, they set their sights on unconquered lands to both the north and the south.

Among these southern lands was the area soon to be called Nicaragua. The first conquistador to explore the region with the intent of colonizing it in the name of Spain was Gil González Dávila, in 1522. He and his men encountered several groups of indigenous people. After trying to force the Roman Catholic religion on these people while gathering gold and other valuable resources, the Spaniards were driven from the area.

Christopher Columbus led four voyages to the Americas between 1492 and 1504.

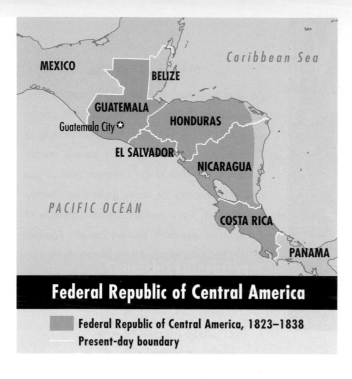

Federal Republic of Central America

Federal Republic of Central America, 1823–1838
Present-day boundary

Independence

Beginning in the mid-1700s, many of the European nations that had colonized the Americas were beginning to lose their influence. A series of struggles between these nations not only weakened them at home but also loosened their stranglehold on many of their distant colonies. The United States broke from British rule during the American Revolution. In Nicaragua and neighboring nations, a similar feeling of independence was brewing.

Many in the region were tired of Spanish rule, and some were tired of the sometimes heavy presence of the Catholic Church. In 1821, both Mexico and most of Central America declared itself free of Spanish control. Mexico tried to incorporate Central America into one state, but the Central Americans refused. So, in 1823, the Federal Republic of Central America was established. It included what are now Guatemala, El Salvador, Honduras, Nicaragua, and Costa Rica.

Despite their good intentions, the next few years were fraught with tension among these countries. By 1838, Nicaragua had withdrawn from the Federal Republic of Central America and become an independent nation.

Independence did not bring peace, however. Granada was the center of the conservative movement in the country, while the people who controlled León were more liberal.

The two groups fought for control, sometimes violently. The British, meanwhile, had seized a stretch of land along the Caribbean coast.

William Walker (holding paper) meets with representatives of the Federal Republic of Central America in 1856.

The United States Gets Involved

The United States played an important role in the history of Nicaragua starting in the 1850s. In 1855, an American named William Walker arrived in Nicaragua and became involved in the ongoing battle between conservative and liberal factions. Walker came out in support of the liberal side and was soon commanding his own forces. In late 1855, he and his across Nicaragua connecting the Atlantic and the Pacific Oceans. In 1909, the United States sent military forces to Nicaragua. Realizing that the United States planned to undermine his leadership, Zelaya left Nicaragua that same year.

After Zelaya exited, Nicaragua was led once again by conservatives, particularly the Chamorro family, for the next sixteen years. The conservatives were generally friendly toward the United States and put up little resistance when the U.S. government sent military forces to occupy the country in order to protect its economic interests.

A civil war between the conservative and liberal factions erupted again in May 1926. The United States intervened and forced a truce, but it was not the end of the matter. A liberal general named Augusto César Sandino vowed to carry on in order to overthrow the conservative government and eliminate U.S. interference in Nicaragua once and for all. The United States decided to withdraw all military forces from Nicaragua in 1933. Sandino was assassinated the following year.

Augusto Sandino (center) strongly resisted U.S. involvement in Nicaragua, making him a hero to many in his country.

The Somoza Era

In January 1937, following an election in December 1936 that was almost certainly fixed in his favor, Anastasio Somoza

Many people in Nicaragua opposed the Somozas' long and brutal dictatorship. Nicaraguans battle police by throwing rocks during an antigovernment demonstration in 1963.

Some in Nicaragua hoped the assassination would mark the end of the Somozan tyranny, but Somoza's son Luis took power immediately. Like his father, Luis Somoza had a strong relationship with the United States and maintained the status quo. The same was true of Anastasio Jr., who took over after Luis died of a heart attack in 1967. By this time, however, many Nicaraguans had had enough of the Somoza dynasty, and the winds of change were beginning to blow.

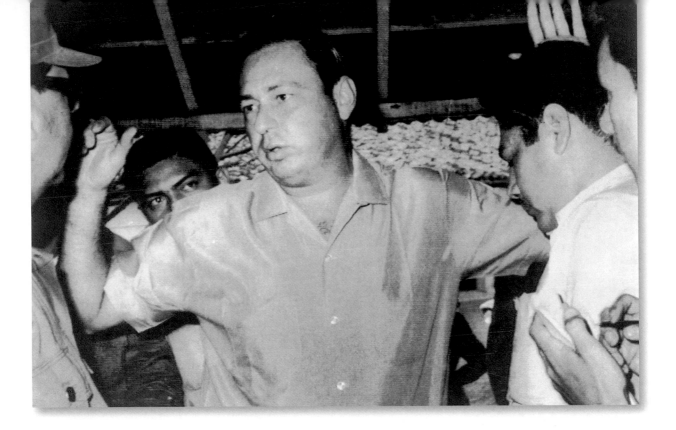

The Sandinistas

In the 1960s, several new political parties formed in Nicaragua. One of them was the Sandinista National Liberation Front, more commonly known as the Sandinistas. The party took its name from Augusto César Sandino, the liberal general who refused to bend to conservative rule and American influence. Until the early 1970s, the Sandinistas had varying degrees of success in gaining support from Nicaraguans. They also gained some support from outsiders such as the Cuban government. Cuba was a communist nation, meaning the government owned the businesses and controlled the economy, and many Sandinistas favored this system. Many pro-Somoza groups, including the U.S. government, viewed the Sandinistas as little more than brutal revolutionaries.

Pedro Joaquín Chamorro was the publisher of *La Prensa*, the only major newspaper to oppose the Somoza regime. In 1967, the government had him arrested in the weeks before the election of Anastasio Somoza Jr.

Nicaraguans sort through debris following the 1972 earthquake. The quake left a quarter of a million people homeless.

Their power began to change in late 1972, when the country was struck by a massive earthquake that killed more than ten thousand people in the capital city of Managua alone. When the government of Anastasio Somoza Jr. took much of the aid money sent from other countries for themselves, the Sandinistas, buoyed by public outrage, took action. In the years that followed, their credibility on the world stage rose, while that of the corrupt Somoza government fell. Even U.S. president Jimmy Carter began to question the validity of the Somoza regime. In 1979, the Sandinistas succeeded in removing Anastasio Somoza Jr. from power. It was the first time in more than forty years that the Nicaraguan government wasn't ruled in some way by a member of the Somoza family.

Changing Economy

Soon after taking control of the Nicaraguan government, the Sandinista leadership began focusing on a reconstruction program aimed at repairing much of the damage the Somozas had done to the Nicaraguan people. In the middle of the century, farmers had begun to grow a wider variety of crops while trying to improve their technology. Farming methods had advanced the world over, and Nicaragua had fallen behind. Still, by the 1960s, Nicaraguans were producing more on their land than ever before. Crops such as fruits, sugar, coffee, and cotton were being exported in huge quantities. Food processing was also becoming a major source of income.

Sandinistas celebrate the end of the Somoza regime in 1979.

Daniel Ortega was a member of the Sandinista leadership that took power in 1979. He was elected president in 1984.

When the Sandinistas took power, the Nicaraguan economy went through radical changes. The Sandinistas promoted socialism, a system in which the government controls major industries and land for the benefit of all citizens. Sandinista leaders promised that there would be much greater economic equality than under the Somoza regime, with opportunities for even the poorest citizens. They seized properties formerly owned by the Somozas and began programs designed to spread wealth to everyone while spurring new growth in every part of the economy. Unfortunately, this approach did not produce the desired results. The United States, which had supported the Somozas and been involved in many joint commercial interests, cut ties with the Sandinistas. The Sandinistas sought financial support from the communist Soviet Union, a large country in Asia and eastern Europe that broke up in 1991, becoming Russia and more than a dozen other nations. But the payments from the Soviets were just a fraction of what the Nicaraguans needed. The economy suffered, and prices rose rapidly. By the mid-1980s, the government was forced to enact price controls.

The Ortega Years

One of the leaders of this period was a rising star in the Sandinista Party named Daniel Ortega. Ortega was born into relative poverty and grew to loathe the elitist Somozas. He and two of his brothers joined the Sandinista movement. While still in his teens, Daniel Ortega traveled to Cuba and became a skilled guerrilla fighter. After returning home, his natural political skills led him to become one of the party's most influential figures. He was elected president in 1984 and took office early the next year.

Ortega's presidency was threatened early on when the United States, under the leadership of President Ronald Reagan, funded an effort by an opposition group known as the Contras to drive Ortega and his party from power. The Contras had bases in border areas of Honduras and Costa Rica. From there, they attacked the Sandinista government. Nicaragua was plunged into another bloody civil war, but Ortega remained in power.

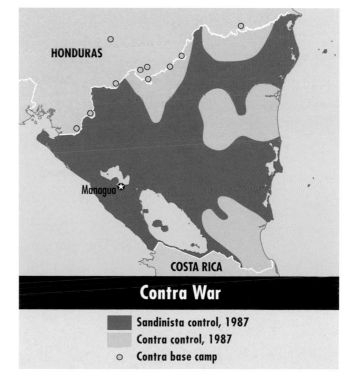

Contra War

- Sandinista control, 1987
- Contra control, 1987
- ○ Contra base camp

Violeta Chamorro

In 1990, Nicaragua opened a new chapter in its history by electing its first female president—Violeta Barrios Torres de Chamorro. Born in 1929 to a family of wealthy landowners who lived near the Costa Rican border, she was a bright student who did well in school and was eventually sent to the United States, where she mastered English. She married Pedro Chamorro in 1950, and two years later Pedro took over his family's newspaper, *La Prensa*, and began getting in trouble for writing articles against the oppressive Somoza regime. In 1978, Pedro was assassinated. His death was an important factor in the Sandinistas' revolutionary campaign against Somoza. In the years ahead, Violeta Chamorro gradually gained power and respect in the government and with the people. However her wealthy background proved challenging to those who saw her as out of touch with ordinary people.

Nevertheless, she was picked as the candidate for the National Opposition Union—a group of several political parties that all agreed that the Contra War needed to end. She proved popular enough to win the

presidency over Daniel Ortega. This made her the first woman to be elected president of a Latin American country. She dedicated her time in office to leading the country into the first sustained peace it had known in decades. She left office in 1997 and continued her dedication to maintaining peace in the region.

Changing Times

The 1990s saw the election of a new president—Violeta Chamorro—and a new set of economic policies. Chamorro moved the nation away from socialism and back toward a more privatized, free-market economy. She hoped this would help rekindle productivity. Another hope was that foreign nations would be interested in investing in Nicaragua again. Instead, outside investors waited to see how the new plan would play out. Prices stopped rising so rapidly, and the

economy became more stable. But the economy did not grow quickly enough, and there were not enough jobs. The already frustrated Nicaraguans grew impatient, and thousands organized strikes in protest. By year 2000, it was clear that another new approach was required.

Even after losing the presidency to Chamorro in 1990, Daniel Ortega remained a major figure in Nicaraguan politics. He worked to make the system of government more democratic than it had ever been. In 2006, he was elected president once again. He has remained in that post ever since. As president, he has continued to pursue socialist policies on many domestic matters, and Nicaragua continues to have a strained relationship with the United States.

Trucks block a road near Managua during a transportation strike in 2008. Truck, bus, and taxi drivers were objecting to rising fuel costs.

CHAPTER 5

The Leadership

NICARAGUA IS A REPRESENTATIVE DEMOCRACY. Like the United States, it emphasizes civil liberties such as the rights to free speech, to vote, and to pursue a career of your own choosing. The government is run according to the principles outlined in the nation's constitution. The most recent version of the Nicaraguan Constitution went into effect in 1987, and it has been amended, or changed, many times since then. Like the U.S. government, Nicaragua's government is divided into three distinct sections in order to assure that no one part has too much power. These three branches of government are the executive, the legislative, and the judicial.

Opposite: **Daniel Ortega began his second tenure as president in 2007.**

The National Flag

The national flag of Nicaragua consists of two horizontal bars of blue along the top and bottom of the flag, with a bar of white sandwiched between them. In the center of the white bar is Nicaragua's emblem—a triangle with the words *Republica de Nicaragua - America Central*—in a circle around it in gold letters. Within the triangle is a rainbow, which symbolizes peace; an ancient kind of hat called a Phrygian cap, which symbolizes freedom; and a chain of five volcanoes, which symbolizes the powerful bond between the countries that made up the Federal Republic of Central America—Costa Rica, El Salvador, Guatemala, Honduras, and Nicaragua. The flags of all five of these countries have

two blue stripes with a white stripe in between, which is based upon the original flag of the Federal Republic of Central America. Nicaragua's flag was officially adopted in 1971.

Executive Branch

The primary function of the executive branch is to oversee the daily management of domestic affairs, and to act as the top representative of the country to the international community. The head of Nicaragua's executive branch is the president. Although many countries have a president, in many cases this is a ceremonial job and the actual leader of the government is the prime minister. In countries such as Nicaragua and the United States, however, the role of president is the most powerful position.

The president is assisted by a vice president and a cabinet. The cabinet is made up of the heads of each major government department. Nicaragua has more than a dozen cabinet departments, including defense, education, agriculture, finance, environment, industry, and labor. The leaders of each of these

departments, as well as many other important officials within the executive branch, are picked by the president and confirmed by the National Assembly, the lawmaking part of the government. Once confirmed, cabinet ministers have a large amount of independence, although they are still expected to conform to national policy.

The Nicaraguan president and vice president hold office for five-year terms. In the past, the president was limited to two terms. However, in 2014, a bill was introduced permitting Ortega to run for a third term in 2016. Members of opposition parties were outraged, considering it nothing more than a way to extend Ortega's power. The bill was approved by the National Assembly. The vote was sixty-four in favor and twenty-five against. Sixty-three of the sixty-four votes in favor of the bill came from members of Ortega's Sandinista Party.

An elderly man casts his vote during an election in Managua in 2012. In Nicaragua, people gain the right to vote at age sixteen.

Nicaragua's National Government

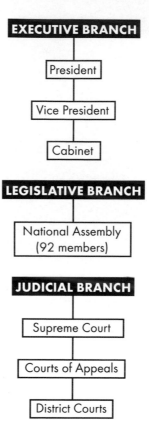

EXECUTIVE BRANCH

President

Vice President

Cabinet

LEGISLATIVE BRANCH

National Assembly
(92 members)

JUDICIAL BRANCH

Supreme Court

Courts of Appeals

District Courts

Legislative Branch

The legislative branch of the Nicaraguan government is the
National Assembly. It serves roughly the same function as
the U.S. Congress, but unlike the U.S. Congress, it has only
one chamber. Nicaragua's National Assembly has ninety-two
members. Of those, ninety are elected by the public. Seventy
of those seats are elected by people in different geographic
regions. Another twenty seats are elected on a nationwide

basis. The final two National Assembly seats are occupied by the nation's previous president and whoever came in second place in the last presidential election.

The National Assembly meets in Managua.

Members of the National Assembly serve five-year terms. The members have the power to enact new laws through a majority vote, and they can also override presidential vetoes. The National Assembly also has the power to approve or reject presidential appointees. In addition, the assembly is responsible for practical matters such as the maintenance of the national budget and the creation of new departments and committees.

Daniel Ortega stands next to Aminta Granera, the head of Nicaragua's national police force. Nicaragua is a relatively safe country, with the lowest murder rate in Central America.

Judicial Branch

The judicial branch of government is the court system. The Nicaraguan court system has multiple levels, including local courts, district courts, and courts of appeals, which review cases that have already been ruled on by lower courts. The highest body is the Supreme Court, which has sixteen members. Its members are chosen by the National Assembly and serve five-year terms.

Nicaragua's judicial branch also includes a military section. The military judiciary handles all matters involving members of the military. The regular civilian court system handles both criminal and civil cases, as well as administrative and constitutional cases.

The National Anthem

Nicaragua's national anthem is "Salve a ti, Nicaragua," or "Hail to Thee, Nicaragua." The music dates back many centuries, and no one knows who composed it. The lyrics were written by poet Salomón Ibarra Mayorga. The song was formally adopted as the national anthem in 1971.

Spanish lyrics

¡Salve a ti, Nicaragua!
En tu suelo, ya no ruge la voz del canon,
ni se tiñe con sangre de hermanos
tu glorioso pendón bicolor.

Brille hermosa la paz en tu cielo,
nada empañe tu gloria inmortal,
¡que el trabajo es tu digno laurel
y el honor es tu enseña triunfal!

English translation

Hail to thee, Nicaragua!
On thy land roars the voice of the cannon no more,
nor does the blood of brothers now stain
thy glorious bicolor banner.

Let us shine beautifully in thy sky,
and nothing dims your immortal glory,
for work is thy well earned laurel
and honor is thy triumphal emblem!

Military

Like most other nations, Nicaragua has a military that protects its borders and keeps its citizens safe. Nicaragua's military has three branches—the army ground forces, the navy, and the air force. Together, they are known as the Nicaraguan Armed Forces. The army ground forces include the regular army as well as the border patrol and the national militia. The air force is small, with only about three dozen craft and a few thousand members. The navy is also small. It is charged with protecting the Nicaraguan shoreline as well as its harbors and shipping lanes.

Nicaraguan soldiers take part in a parade celebrating the founding of the Nicaraguan army. About fourteen thousand people serve in the Nicaraguan military.

Political Parties

Nicaragua has many political parties. The most powerful is the Sandinista National Liberation Front (FSLN), the party of President Daniel Ortega. The Sandinistas were established in 1961. At the time, they argued in favor of communism. They have since moved more toward the center. They now support a mild form of socialism that appeals to the majority of the population.

Other prominent parties include the Independent Liberal Party and the Constitutionalist Liberal Party. The Conservative

Sandinista supporters gather each year to celebrate the anniversary of the revolution that ended the Somoza dictatorship.

Party is Nicaragua's oldest political organization, but it now struggles to gain influence. The Conservatives have had to ally themselves with other minor parties in recent years in order to reach the public. Another party, the Sandinista Renovation Movement, was organized in 1995 by Sandinistas who did not agree with Ortega's abandonment of revolutionary ideals and communism.

The Capital City

Nicaragua's capital city of Managua is located in the western half of the country along the shores of Lake Managua. It was founded in 1819 and became the capital in 1852. The name comes from the Nahuatl term *mana-ahuac*, which means "by the water." The climate in Managua, while a bit on the hot side, remains remarkably consistent, with the average high between 87°F (31°C) and 94°F (34°C) throughout the year. In the dry season, Managua may go a whole month without rain. In the heart of the wet season, however, it can rain every other day.

As the hub of the nation, Managua is also the hub of the nation's economy, with factories producing every-

thing from shoes and clothing to food, electronics, and medicines. The city has also grown in recent years, with new apartment complexes, museums, restaurants, and office buildings being built. The government has also worked to repair roads, bridges, and water systems.

Managua is also Nicaragua's educational and cultural center. Popular sites include the Old Cathedral (above) and the National Palace of Culture, which houses the National Museum and the National Library.

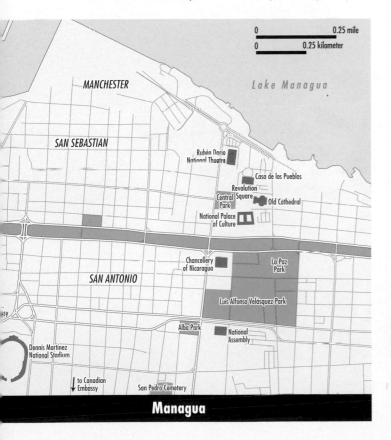

Managua

CHAPTER 6

Economic Matters

WHEN DANIEL ORTEGA WAS ELECTED PRESIDENT again in 2006, he began reforming the economy. He expanded opportunities for loans, which led to an expansion of private businesses. He gave incentives for women to join the workforce, which utilized more talent and energy and increased the size of the nation's economy. He improved working conditions and supported legislation that increased workers' rights. Ortega has also tried to open new markets by building relationships with other countries, including the United States. Ortega's policies have led to gains in some areas, and there are signs of steady growth. But Nicaragua continues to struggle as one of the poorest nations in Central America.

Nicaragua has a labor force of about three million people. Half of them draw their paychecks from the service sector. About a third of workers are employed in agriculture. The

Opposite: **A Nicaraguan man picks plantains, a popular food in Nicaragua. Many of the plantains intended for export are grown in the southern part of the country.**

Money Facts

The basic unit of money in Nicaragua is the córdoba. The córdoba is divided into one hundred centavos. Coins come in values of 5, 10, 25, and 50 centavos as well as 1, 5, and 10 córdobas. Paper currency includes values of 10, 20, 50, 100, 200, and 500 córdobas. Each bill has a different dominant culture and includes images of historical sites or scenes from nature. For example, the 500-córdoba note is pink and features the Cathedral of León on the front and Momotombo volcano on the back. In 2016, 1 córdoba equaled 3 U.S. cents, and US$1.00 equaled 29 córdobas.

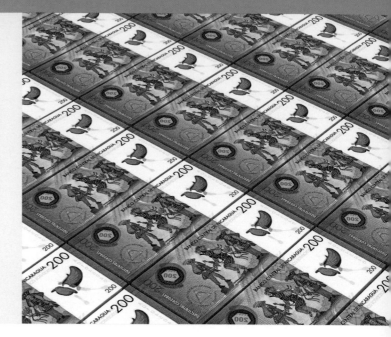

remaining workers are employed in industry. The average Nicaraguan worker makes about $5,000 per year. Despite growth in the economy, about three out of every ten Nicaraguans live in poverty.

A worker carries sugarcane, one of Nicaragua's top products.

Coffee beans are often dried before they are hulled and sorted.

What Nicaragua Grows, Makes, and Mines

AGRICULTURE (2012)

Sugarcane	6,718,247 metric tons
Corn	471,000 metric tons
Coffee	107,000 metric tons

MANUFACTURING (VALUE ADDED, 2012)

Food products	$850,000,000
Textiles and clothing	$145,000,000
Machinery	$73,000,000

MINING (2012)

Silver	about 13,000 kilograms
Gold	about 9,000 kilograms
Gypsum	46,570 metric tons

A man pulls a cart of plantains through the town of Jinotepe, west of Granada.

Agriculture

About one-fifth of Nicaragua's economy comes from things grown in the earth. Some crops are grown primarily for export. These include sugarcane and coffee. Products grown that are mostly consumed by Nicaraguans include corn, beans, rice, and plantains, a kind of starchy banana. Many fruits and vegetables are also grown.

Raising livestock is an important business in Nicaragua. Cattle are raised for both meat and dairy products. Some Nicaraguans raise goats, hogs, and sheep as well.

Manufacturing and Mining

Industry has been growing in recent times and now accounts for about a quarter of the nation's gross domestic product, the total value of all the goods and services produced there. Factories in Nicaragua turn out such goods as clothing, shoes, chemicals, and food products. Nicaragua also produces petroleum products. Construction is a growing business.

Nicaragua has a small mining industry. Miners remove gold and silver from beneath the earth. The country also has deposits of zinc, copper, and iron.

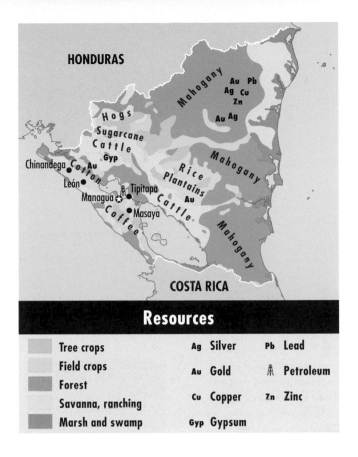

Resources

Tree crops	Ag Silver	Pb Lead
Field crops	Au Gold	⚒ Petroleum
Forest	Cu Copper	Zn Zinc
Savanna, ranching	Gyp Gypsum	
Marsh and swamp		

Sending It Home

An increasingly important piece to Nicaragua's economic puzzle comes in the form of remittances—money earned by Nicaraguans working in other countries and then sent back home. Many Nicaraguans can make much more money for the same work in another country. So they move to a nation where they can find work and get paid ten, twenty, or even thirty times what they would at home. They keep what they need to live on and send the rest to their families. A single Nicaraguan working abroad can make a big difference in the fortunes of their family back home. Many Nicaraguans go to Costa Rica to find work. Some also go to the United States. Remittances now account for between 10 and 15 percent of Nicaragua's gross domestic product.

Services

About half of Nicaraguan workers are employed in service industries. These include areas such as tourism, health care, education, banking, repair work, telecommunications, restaurants, and sales. Tourism is one of the leading industries in the country now. People come from all over to relax on beautiful beaches, explore colonial cities, climb volcanoes, and hike through misty forests. The tourist industry has grown tremendously in recent years because Nicaragua is inexpensive compared to many other places.

Tourists take part in a sport known as volcano boarding, in which they slide down the ash-covered slope of a volcano. The most popular site for this sport is Cerro Negro, a volcano near León.

Imports and Exports

As the people of Nicaragua earn more and Nicaraguan businesses expand, so grows the need for imported products. Among the most in-demand imports are consumer goods such as electronics and clothing, industrial equipment, building materials such as wood, glass, and concrete, and products such as gasoline. About 16 percent of Nicaragua's imports come from the United States, more than from any other nation. Venezuela and Mexico aren't far behind. Other major import sources include China, Guatemala, El Salvador, and Costa Rica.

Nicaragua exports a broad array of products. These include coffee, cotton, sugar, nuts, tobacco, and fruits. Meat from farm animals such as cows and pigs have increased in importance

A ship laden with huge containers waits to be unloaded at the port in Corinto. Top imports in Nicaragua include oil, medicines, metals, and cars and trucks.

A gold miner in La Libertad, east of Managua. Gold is one of Nicaragua's major exports.

in recent years. Gold is the top mineral product exported. A lot of seafood is exported from Nicaragua, including lobster, shrimp, salmon, sturgeon, snapper, grouper, and paddlefish. Automobile parts are exported, as are textiles such as clothing, towels, and blankets. About half of all Nicaraguan exports go to the United States. Many Nicaraguan products also end up in Mexico and Venezuela.

Transportation

Getting around Nicaragua can sometimes be difficult. Major highways include the Inter-American Highway, which runs north-south through Nicaragua and the rest of Central America. There are also major roads connecting Managua to other cities. But there are fewer roads in the less developed eastern part of the country. And everywhere, some highways become impassable during the rainy season.

Boat travel is important on Lake Nicaragua, Lake Managua, the San Juan River, and other bodies of water. Major ports are at Corinto on the Pacific coast and Puerto Cabezas and Bluefields on the Caribbean coast.

Managua is the site of the country's main international airport. Puerto Cabezas and Bluefields also have major airports.

People and trucks pass through a flooded stretch of the Inter-American Highway.

CHAPTER 7

The People

NICARAGUA IS A NATION OF ABOUT SIX MILLION people, roughly as many as live in the state of Maryland. Most people live in the western part of the country, in the lowlands near the lakes. The valleys between the mountains also have large populations. Nearly three out five people live in urban areas, and roughly 40 percent of the people live in the area around Managua, the capital and largest city.

Ethnicity

Nicaragua is a melting pot of people from many different ethnicities. The majority of the population—about two-thirds—is

Population of largest cities (2012 est.)	
Managua	973,087
León	144,538
Masaya	130,113
Tipitapa	127,153
Chinandega	126,387

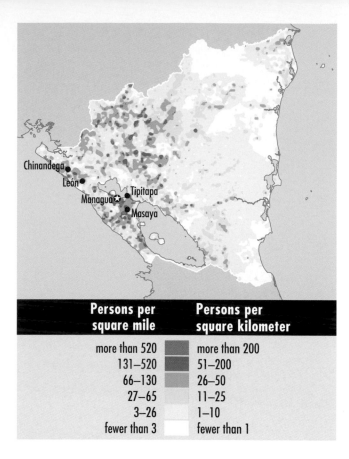

Persons per square mile		Persons per square kilometer
more than 520		more than 200
131–520		51–200
66–130		26–50
27–65		11–25
3–26		1–10
fewer than 3		fewer than 1

Ethnic Background in Nicaragua

Mestizo	69%
White	18%
Black	8%
Amerindian	5%

mestizo, people of mixed European, indigenous, and sometimes African backgrounds.

Roughly 18 percent of Nicaraguans are white, 8 percent are black, and another 5 percent are indigenous. A small percentage of Nicaraguans belong to other races.

Most people of African ancestry live on the Atlantic coast. Many people of indigenous ancestry live near the Caribbean coast in the eastern half of the country. The largest of these groups is the Miskito, most of whom have both African and indigenous backgrounds. About 120,000 Miskito live in Nicaragua today. Most make their living through agriculture, hunting, and fishing.

Coming and Going

Immigrants make up about only 1 percent of Nicaragua's population. For many people, Nicaragua is not a desirable place to move to because road conditions are poor, there are few jobs, and some rural areas lack electricity. On the other hand, there has been a small increase in the immigration of retirees from other nations, including the United States. They are drawn by Nicaragua's low cost of living and low crime rate.

A larger number of Nicaraguans have left their homeland

behind to start a new life elsewhere. It is believed that around 1.8 million Nicaraguans live in other countries. Most move looking for work, with the largest numbers going to Costa Rica and the United States. Many also live in El Salvador and Honduras.

Most black Nicaraguans live along the Caribbean coast.

Language

Many different languages are spoken in Nicaragua every day. Spanish, the country's official language, is the most widespread, used by about 4.5 million of the nation's 6 million people. Nicaraguans speak a particular version of Spanish that has grammar that is sometimes different than standard

Elderly Nicaraguans relax in Granada. On average, Nicaraguans live seventy-three years.

Spanish. Nicaraguan Spanish also incorporates words that can be traced back to the Aztec or Mayan civilizations.

Another language used by many people in Nicaragua is the Miskito language. This language is the most common in the northeast, where the majority of the Miskito population is located. It is also used by many people living over the border in neighboring Honduras. In total, nearly two hundred thousand people speak Miskito.

A growing percentage of Nicaraguans are bilingual, and many can speak English. There are generally two forms used—common English and a variant known as Creole English. Creole English uses English as its base, but has such a strong influence of native languages that it has taken on its own identity.

School

Going to school is free for all Nicaraguan children. Their schooling begins around the age of six or seven with a pre-primary grade, similar to kindergarten, followed by six years of primary education. The grading system in Nicaragua is different than in American schools: 90–100 is a high A (outstanding); 80–89 is a low A (very good); 70–79 is a B (good); 60–69 is a C (regular); and anything 59 or below represents a failing grade.

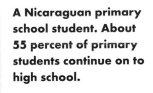

How Do You Say? . . .

Here are some Spanish words and phrases that may come in handy if you ever visit Nicaragua.

Sí	Yes
No	No
Hola	Hello
Adios	Good-bye
Chigüín	Boy
Chigüína	Girl
Bueno	Okay
Tuani	Cool
Púchica	Oops
¿Qué onda?	What's up?
Hay nos vidrios	See you later
Estoy cansado	I'm tired
Buenas noches	Good night
Buenos días	Good morning

A Nicaraguan primary school student. About 55 percent of primary students continue on to high school.

Students in Nicaragua typically wear uniforms to school.

The school year runs from February to November. Although attendance is required, the government is flexible on this point because many children are needed at home to work and help support their families. This is especially true in the agricultural areas, where children often get very little schooling in their youth. In fact, a sizable percentage of Nicaraguan children do not enjoy the benefits of education beyond the sixth grade. This trend has resulted in a labor force that is largely unskilled. Still, 83 percent of Nicaraguans can read and write.

Nicaragua has more than forty different colleges and more than a hundred technical schools. Following graduation, those lucky enough to afford higher education can choose between college studies or vocational or technical training. Few students get this opportunity, and those that do find themselves in great demand in terms of employment. In many cases, only children of the very wealthy have a chance to receive a university education.

The main campus of the National Autonomous University is in Managua. It is the oldest university in the nation, founded in 1812. More than thirty thousand students attend the school.

Students work together at the National Autonomous University of Nicaragua in Managua.

CHAPTER 8

The World of Religion

EVERYONE IN NICARAGUA HAS THE RIGHT TO WORSHIP as they want. It is guaranteed in Nicaragua's constitution. Although Nicaragua has no official religion, Roman Catholicism is the most widespread. Many of the early conquistadores arrived in Nicaragua and neighboring areas with the intent of converting the indigenous people to the Catholic faith. By the early twentieth century, the majority of Nicaraguans had been converted.

Opposite: **Nicaraguan Catholics attend a mass. More than half of Nicaraguans say they attend church services at least once a week.**

The Cathedral of León

Of all the many Spanish-influenced structures in Nicaragua, few are as impressive as the Cathedral of the Assumption of Mary of León, also known as the Cathedral of León. Construction began in 1747 and was not completed until nearly seventy years later. It is one of the most revered Catholic churches in all of Central America. The front facade is particularly breathtaking, featuring carved white stone and square towers on either side. Due to the church's solid construction, it has been able to withstand many earthquakes, volcanic eruptions, and hurricanes. Tunnels beneath the cathedral connect directly with other churches around León. Also under the church are the crypts of many notable figures, including ten bishops. In 2011, UNESCO (the United Nations Educational, Scientific and Cultural Organization) designated it a World Heritage Site, a site of outstanding importance.

Catholicism

For Nicaraguan Catholics, their faith is tightly intertwined with their everyday life. Many attend church services at least once a week and listen with great attention to the declarations of their local bishops. Bishops, leaders in the Catholic Church who oversee a number of different churches, have particular influence in Nicaraguan society. For example, if the government enacts a new policy, it is greatly to its benefit for a bishop to publicly approve that policy. Otherwise, the government may find that citizens are unwilling to accept it. In addition, the pope, the head of the Roman Catholic Church, is considered the final authority on church matters.

Many Nicaraguans exercise their faith by favoring one or more Catholic saints. They feel they can reach God directly by praying to a saint. Similarly, it is not unusual to find images—paintings, sculptures, and medallions—of various saints in Nicaraguan homes or worn on necklaces. Nicaraguans hold many religious celebrations during the course of a year to honor favored saints.

Nicaraguans take part in a religious procession in the city of Jinotega in the Central Highlands. In a 2014 survey, 88 percent of Nicaraguans said religion was very important in their lives.

María Romero Meneses

María Romero Meneses is one of the most notable religious figures in Nicaraguan history. Born in Granada in 1902, Meneses endured a bout of rheumatic fever as a child that threatened her life. Against all odds, she recovered, which inspired her to devote her life to the church and to charitable causes. She moved to Costa Rica in 1931 to become a teacher in an all-girls school. Although her students came from wealthy families, Meneses instilled in them the importance of helping those less fortunate. Many of those students went on to perform great acts of charity in their own right. In her later years, Meneses helped establish health clinics, food banks, and schools for the underprivileged. She died in 1977 after a remarkable life of dedicated compassion.

Protestantism

Protestantism is another form of Christianity, similar to Catholicism in many ways except without the recognition of the pope's authority. The Protestant movement had its origins in the early 1500s, when a faction of the Catholic faith became uncomfortable with certain teachings. Throughout the remainder of the 1500s, Protestantism spread rapidly throughout Europe. When European settlers came to the Western Hemisphere, including Nicaragua, they brought their beliefs with them and tried to influence others to follow their doctrines rather than those of Catholicism.

Protestantism didn't really begin to penetrate Nicaraguan society until the early twentieth century. It began largely on the nation's Caribbean coast, where people belonged to a vari-

Religious Holidays

March or April	Maundy Thursday
March or April	Good Friday
March or April	Holy Saturday
March or April	Easter
November 2	All Saints' Day
December 8	Feast of the Immaculate Conception
December 25	Christmas

ety of different Protestant denominations, or subgroups, which have different beliefs and practices. It has only been in recent times that Protestantism has begun to gain ground in the

Many Nicaraguans bring flowers to their relatives' graves on All Saints' Day.

western half of the country. Common Protestant denominations in Nicaragua include Pentecostal, Episcopalian, Hussite (particularly along the Caribbean coast), Adventist, Baptist, and Jehovah's Witness.

Islam

The Muslim community in Nicaragua is tiny in comparison to those of Catholics and Protestants. Muslims began arriving in Nicaragua in the late 1800s and early 1900s, some escaping upheaval in the Middle East after World War I. More moved to Nicaragua throughout the twentieth century. Many

Protestant Nicaraguans take part in a baptism ceremony on Big Corn Island.

Muslims left Nicaragua after the earthquake of 1972 and during the political turmoil in the years that followed. Today, an estimated 1,500 Muslims live in Nicaragua. The majority of them live in the capital city of Managua.

Muslims pray at a mosque in Nicaragua.

Judaism

Jewish people have lived in Nicaragua through the centuries, though in small numbers. The earliest Jewish settlers came from Europe sometime in the early to mid-1800s. Another wave arrived in the late 1920s, settling in and around the capital city of Managua. Many left after the Sandinistas came to power. In recent years, some Jews have returned, but their numbers are still very small, at only about one hundred.

Major Religions in Nicaragua	
Roman Catholic	58%
Protestant	25%
No religion	15%
Other	2%

CHAPTER 9

A Dynamic Culture

THE LITERARY TRADITIONS OF NICARAGUA STRETCH back many centuries, long before the arrival of the Spanish conquistadores. As a nation of storytellers, Nicaraguans have told their tales not just through literature but also through dance, music, and art. Many stories have been passed down orally, a rich tradition that continues to this day.

Opposite: **A masked folk dancer takes part in a festival in Granada.**

A depiction of the cart from the story "La Carreta Nagua"

Mythology and Folklore

Some of the most enduring stories Nicaraguans tell are myths and folktales that are grounded in some elements of reality.

"La Carreta Nagua," for example, is the story of a rattling wooden cart driven by Death himself and pulled by two ghostly oxen—one dark and one white—down the

Witchy Woman

La Cegua is a witchlike being who can take on many forms and perform acts such as flying, walking on water, and passing through solid objects such as walls. She haunts men during the night, particularly those who have not shown enough respect or consideration for the women in their life. According to legend, she is the ghost of a woman who suffered greatly under the influence of a handsome man who never truly cared for her but enjoyed toying with her feelings. After dying of a broken heart, she came back as an angry specter who attacks men of questionable faithfulness. She does not harm them physically, but instead speaks words of such horrific impact that the men lose their minds and never recover.

Nicaraguan streets during the night. If the cart stops at a particular home, that means one of its residents will die soon—maybe even someone who seemed to be in good health. While the origins of "La Carreta Nagua" have been lost in time, there is a theory that the story stems from the carts driven by European slavers who snatched family members away during the night to labor in fields and mines until they'd been worked to death.

"El Cadejo" is a legend told in many Latin American countries, each with its own variation. In Nicaragua, el cadejo is a pair of huge, shaggy dogs that accompany travelers during the night. One is white and the other black. The white one symbolizes goodness and will protect the travelers, whereas the black one preys on them. Once the travelers reach their destination, the dogs will continue on to the horizon until they disappear. If they fight, the white dog will always drive off the black one, but neither will ever kill the other, underscoring the endless battle between good and evil. It is possible the idea for "El Cadejo" originated in Mexico, where dogs figure prominently in religion and folklore.

The National Museum of Nicaragua is located in the National Palace of Culture in Managua.

passed his love for visual art on to his son, who then studied art in the United States and Mexico while still a young man. He was influenced by both the impressionists, who painted the effects of light on objects, and expressionists, who expressed their emotional response to objects and events in

Asilia Guillén

Asilia Guillén is a central figure in Nicaragua's art heritage, one of the leaders of the primitivism movement that arose in the 1950s. At first, Guillén's main interest was not so much in painting but in the fine art of embroidery. Rodrigo Peñalba became familiar with her embroidery work and urged her to do similar work on canvas. Like Peñalba, she chose the immediate world around her as her subjects—people, landscapes, and objects. Her work has enjoyed increasing appreciation in recent times. Her bold, bright paintings are now recognized as a forerunner of the styles that many Nicaraguan artists employ today.

paint. Peñalba's work was characterized by bold contrasts and often striking pastel colors. Two of his favorite subjects were the Nicaraguan landscape and Nicaraguan women. Most of Peñalba's notable work is in the form of murals, which continue to be one of the top art forms in the country today. Many consider Peñalba the Father of Modern Art in Nicaragua.

There are many painters in the Solentiname Islands. They often depict lush, personal views of the landscape around them.

A group of men play marimbas at an event in southern Nicaragua.

Music

Most Nicaraguan music features percussion, guitars, horns, and the marimba, which is Nicaragua's national instrument. A marimba looks very much like a xylophone, although the keys are more commonly made from wood than metal. The marimbist strikes the keys with mallets, which are similar to drumsticks, but with a rounded head about the size of a golf ball on one end. The player usually holds one mallet in each hand, but sometimes advanced marimbists hold two mallets in each hand. The marimba produces a beautiful woody sound.

The marimba is most popular in the western half of the country. Along the eastern coast, however, drums and strong rhythms are more dominant. In this part of the country, the music has a Caribbean influence that makes it more intense. One of the unique styles in the eastern region is called Palo de Mayo (Maypole), which features prominently in the annual Palo de Mayo festival that takes place at the beginning of May. Modern Palo de Mayo music often features electronic instruments rather than the more traditional instruments.

Nicaraguans listen to many types of music from around the world. People listen to the latest rock and hip-hop music from the United States, for example. Reggae, which comes from the Caribbean island nation of Jamaica, and music from other Latin American countries are also very popular.

Drums are used in many kinds of music in Nicaragua.

Dance

Dancing is one of the most practiced and celebrated forms of expression in Nicaragua. Dancing involves people from all walks of life—young, old, male, and female. To perform traditional dances, Nicaraguans often dress in brightly colored costumes. Many of these dances tell a story, often with a powerful underlying theme. These dances represent the deep traditions of the Nicaraguan culture, and many have been performed for centuries.

Girls dance in a parade in Granada.

Perhaps the best-known Nicaraguan dance is El Güegüense. This is not merely a dance, but a combination of dance, music, and theater that come together to tell a remarkable tale. The story itself dates back to the 1500s and tells of a Nicaraguan businessperson who attempts to evade paying taxes to the Spanish government by trying to arrange a marriage between his son and the daughter of a high-ranking Spanish official. It is considered a comedy, but with strong undertones of the resentment that indigenous Nicaraguans felt toward the Spanish conquerors in the early colonial days. It is performed in many parts of the country, but is particularly associated with the southwestern town of Diriamba, where it is thought to have originated. The piece is such a defining statement of Nicaraguan culture that UNESCO declared it a "Masterpiece of the Oral and Intangible Heritage of Humanity."

People typically wear elaborate costumes when performing El Güegüense.

Sports

Like people in countries around the world, Nicaraguan people enjoy sports. Soccer, known as *fútbol* (football) in Spanish, is tremendously popular. The simplicity of it—all you need is a field, a ball, and some players—means that people of all economic backgrounds can enjoy it. No special equipment is necessary. The Nicaraguan national team, known as the Blue and White because of the colors of their uniforms, competes against other national teams. Though they've never made it to the World Cup, the world's premier soccer tournament,

Dennis Martínez National Stadium

There are many sports stadiums in Nicaragua, but the best known is currently named after Dennis Martínez. Martínez represented everything that aspiring young athletes dream about in Nicaragua. Born in Granada in 1955, he dreamed of playing professional baseball as a young boy and displayed remarkable talent as a pitcher. In 1976, he was signed by the Baltimore Orioles, becoming the first Nicaraguan to play major league baseball in the United States. Over the next twelve years, he was the winning pitcher in an impressive 245 games. In July 1991, he made the record books when he pitched the thirteenth perfect game in major league baseball history, meaning he pitched an entire game without giving up a hit or walking a batter.

The Dennis Martínez National Stadium is located in Managua. It hosts not just baseball games and other sporting events, but also religious events and other festivals. The stadium was originally built in 1948 and called the National Stadium. After it was destroyed in the 1972 earthquake it was rebuilt and had various names through the years. Then, in 1998, the stadium was renamed in Martínez's honor.

they have done well in other tournaments, and Nicaraguans are always ready to show their support.

Baseball is also extremely popular in Nicaragua. Baseball has been played in the country since the late 1800s, when a visiting American businessman introduced it. By the 1970s,

In Nicaragua, baseball is popular among both children and adults.

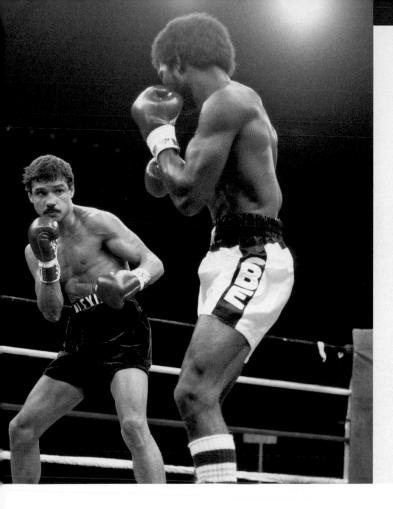

Another sport enjoyed by many Nicaraguans is boxing. It held only moderate interest in the country until a Managuan named Alexis Argüello (far left) came onto the scene in the late 1960s. Throughout the 1970s and into the 1980s, he maintained a stunning record that led him to world titles in featherweight, super featherweight, and lightweight classes. His nickname *El Flaco Explosivo*—the explosive thin man—underscored the remarkable amount of power that came from his relatively thin body. Many boxing experts consider him among the best in history, and his achievements spurred great interest in the sport among Nicaraguans.

Argüello retired from boxing a national hero. He became involved in politics and was elected mayor of Managua in 2008. He died the following year.

the Nicaraguan national team had won several medals in the Baseball World Cup, inspiring great national pride as well as increased interest in the sport among youngsters. In 1976, pitcher Dennis Martínez became the first Nicaraguan to play in the U.S. major leagues. In the years since, a large number of players have been signed by U.S. major league teams, including pitcher Vicente Padilla and shortstop Everth Cabrera.

Nicaragua also has its own professional baseball organization, the Nicaraguan Professional Baseball League, which was founded in 1956. The best players in the league are considered the very best in all of Latin America.

CHAPTER 10

Family and Friends

FOR THE AVERAGE NICARAGUAN, FAMILY SITS AT THE very core of their life. It is not merely a group of relatives who share the same household, but rather a strong and reliable structure that extends well into Nicaraguan society and impacts everything a person does. In Nicaragua, family is more than just parents and children. Children grow up seeing their grandparents, aunts and uncles, cousins, and godparents on a frequent basis. Elders are considered wise and worldly, and youngsters are expected to accord them great respect.

Opposite: **Nicaraguan boys in Granada. About half the people in Nicaragua are under age twenty-five.**

Stronger Together

Family members tend to be open with one another, and when someone is in trouble, that member can depend on the family to help. Similarly, when one family member achieves success in the working world, it is expected that he or she will help relatives do likewise. Thus, there is loyalty within a Nicaraguan

Many Nicaraguans are close to their extended family.

A Nicaraguan Wedding

Since the majority of Nicaraguans are Catholic, most of their weddings follow Catholic traditions. A couple getting married has the choice of having a small, secular ceremony or holding it in a church as part of a larger mass. The larger church weddings are more popular, as church services are a regular part of the lives of many Nicaraguans and such a ceremony emphasizes the celebratory feel of the occasion.

During the mass, the priest reads passages from the Bible and may give a sermon on the importance of a strong and respectful union. Then the actual wedding takes place, where the bride and groom exchange vows and rings. The priest blesses the rings before they are placed on the couple's fingers. The bride may also follow an old Nicaraguan custom by placing a single rose at the feet of the statue of Mary, the mother of Jesus. Guests may also bring small gifts to the altar to honor the couple. The priest reads the Prayer of the Faithful, and the mass continues. At the end of the service, the priest presents the newly married couple to the audience, who responds with cheers and applause.

family, and with that comes a strong sense of stability. The reputation of a family is also important. Nicaraguans believe that when one person does something shameful, it reflects badly on everyone in their home.

It is not unusual for a newly married couple to move back into the home of one of their parents, at least until they can afford to move into a home of their own. Other family members may contribute money to help a young family get their own home, as family money is considered just that—belonging to everyone.

Public Holidays

January 1	New Year's Day
March or April	Holy Thursday
March or April	Good Friday
May 1	Labor Day
July 19	Sandinista Revolution Day
September 14	San Jacinto Day
September 15	Independence Day
December 8	Feast of the Immaculate Conception
December 25	Christmas Day

Families tend to be larger in agricultural regions than in urban areas, because in farming communities it is helpful to have more children who can work on the farms. Throughout Nicaragua, women have two children on average.

Revelers wear masks during a New Year's Day parade in Nicaragua.

Cuisine

Nicaraguans have, for the most part, a healthy diet. They eat many fruits and vegetables, as well as rice and beans. The most common item in the Nicaraguan diet is corn. It has been grown in the country for hundreds of years and is integrated into an astonishing variety of dishes. Two other dietary staples are rice and beans, which are also incredibly versatile. Many meals also include some variety of plantains or bananas. Fried plantains, for example, are very popular. Corn, rice, beans, and plantains are easy to grow, inexpensive to purchase, and are widely available.

Corn is eaten in many forms in Nicaragua, including roasted corn on the cob and tortillas.

Gallo Pinto

One of the most popular meals in Nicaragua is also one of the simplest, a rice and bean dish called *gallo pinto,* which means "spotted rooster." It may be so named, because the colors and look of the dish resemble the feathers of some roosters. Have an adult help you with this recipe.

Ingredients

½ pound red beans

2 cloves garlic, peeled

½ teaspoon adobo seasoning

¼ cup corn oil

½ medium onion, sliced

2 cups of long-grain rice, cooked

Directions

1. Rinse the beans and then let them soak in water overnight in the refrigerator.
2. Drain the beans and combine them in a pot with the garlic. Cover the beans with water, put the pot on the stovetop, and bring the mixture to a boil. Lower the heat and simmer until the beans are tender. This should take about an hour. Add the adobo seasoning and then continue to simmer for about ten minutes. The beans should be fully tender.
3. Remove the pot from the heat. Let it cool, and then drain the cooking liquid but keep it for later. The garlic can be thrown away.
4. Warm the oil in a skillet on medium heat. Add the onions, and cook until they are translucent but not browned (about five minutes). Then add the beans and continue cooking for five more minutes.
5. Add the precooked rice and continue cooking, stirring often, for another five minutes. As the mixture is cooking, stir in half a cup of the reserved cooking liquid and discard the rest. When the mixture is heated through and has absorbed the liquid, it is ready. Let it cool for another few minutes before serving.

It is not unusual for Nicaraguan families to have a big garden on their property. In their gardens, they grow vegetables such as tomatoes, green beans, peas, Swiss chard, carrots, onions, and different types of peppers. They also grow fruits such as bananas, mangoes, plantains, papayas, oranges, lemons, coconuts, and pineapples. Many Nicaraguans also grow their own herbs, such as cilantro, oregano, basil, and mint. With so many things growing right in the backyard, there is always fresh food.

Nicaraguans include meat in their diet, although it is not always cheap or easily available. Beef, pork, and chicken are the most common. Along the coastal regions, particularly the Pacific coast, fish and shellfish are frequently eaten. Nothing is wasted. Nicaraguans have been known to make meals out of turtles (and their eggs), lizards, snakes, monkeys, and even armadillos.

A wide variety of fruits and vegetables are available in Nicaragua.

A Simple Game of Marbles

One of the most popular games in Nicaragua is marbles, also known as *chibolas*. Marbles are small, brightly colored glass spheres, and children have found countless ways to play with them. One of the most popular games involves drawing a large circle on the ground. A player then shoots a marble from the hand using the thumb, trying to land the marbles inside the circle. Another game involves trying to strike opponents' marbles with the intent of sending those marbles outside the circle. A third requires drawing a series of concentric circles, like a target, with each smaller circle having a higher point value. The object is to shoot a marble as close to dead center as possible, with the winning player accumulating the most points by the end of the game.

Clothing

According to one saying, "You can never be too underdressed in Nicaragua." It is a hot country, so wearing light, comfortable clothing is the best way to dress.

On an ordinary day, a man wears shorts and a comfortable shirt, usually either a T-shirt or a button-down with short sleeves, along with flip-flops or sandals. In particularly humid conditions, it is not unusual for men to take off their tops and go bare-chested. Women also dress in shorts and a short-sleeved shirt or tank top, and they favor light blouses, often in vivid colors and patterns.

Nicaraguans often wear jeans, and sometimes men will put on cotton slacks if they need to dress up for some occasion. Some men wear suits and ties or uniforms to work.

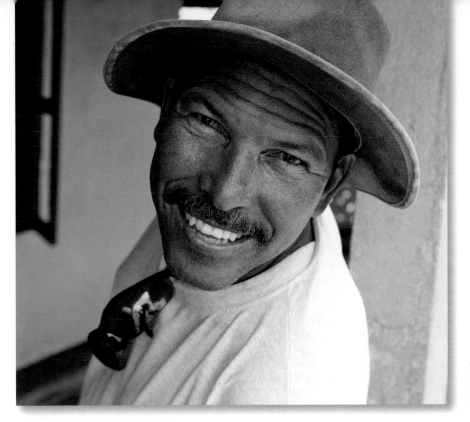

T-shirts and hats are everyday clothes in Nicaragua.

Hats are an easy way to combat the sun, and both men and women like to wear broad-brimmed fedoras. Baseball caps are also common.

Back in Time

Traditional Nicaraguan clothing is quite different from everyday wear. For both men and women, it has a strong Spanish influence. Traditional women's dresses have short sleeves, layered frills, and bright colors. When dressing traditionally, women also wear a headband, a kerchief or hat, and jewelry. A man's traditional costume may consist of something as simple as long white pants and a white short-sleeved shirt. A man might also wear a scarf around his neck, tied at the throat with the two tails hanging down the front.

In many towns and cities in Nicaragua, houses are painted bright colors.

Relaxing Together

Despite the difficulties Nicaragua has faced, the people who live there are known for their warmth, generosity, dedication to tradition, pride in their culture, and willingness to work. Many a visitor has gone into Nicaraguan society worried about images they remember in the news showing a war-torn nation weary of a struggling economy and little governmental stability. Many are surprised when they realize the average Nicaraguan citizen seems almost oblivious to the turmoil of the past and goes about his or her daily business with a quiet, steady dignity.

Nicaraguans cherish many of the same values as people anywhere else in the world. They place great importance on family, religion, and staying productive. They can be cautious where outsiders are concerned. Once they are relaxed and comfortable, however, they are willing to open up and enjoy the company of others. Most Nicaraguans enjoy the pleasure of good conversation and are curious about life in other countries. They generally take life as it comes. In a nation where there has been so much difficulty, they are able to find happiness in the simple pleasures of family and friends.

A traveler shows Nicaraguan children pictures on her camera.

Timeline

	ca. 2500 BCE	The Egyptians build the pyramids and the Sphinx in Giza.
	ca. 563 BCE	The Buddha is born in India.
People first settle in what is now Nicaragua. **500s BCE**	**313 CE**	The Roman emperor Constantine legalizes Christianity.
	610	The Prophet Muhammad begins preaching a new religion called Islam.
	1054	The Eastern (Orthodox) and Western (Roman Catholic) Churches break apart.
	1095	The Crusades begin.
	1215	King John seals the Magna Carta.
	1300s	The Renaissance begins in Italy.
	1347	The plague sweeps through Europe.
	1453	Ottoman Turks capture Constantinople, conquering the Byzantine Empire.
	1492	Columbus arrives in North America.
Christopher Columbus sails along the eastern coast of Central America. **1502**	**1500s**	Reformers break away from the Catholic Church, and Protestantism is born.
Spaniard Gil González Dávila explores Nicaragua. **1522**		
Conquistador Francisco Hernández de Córdoba conquers Nicaragua; Granada, the first Spanish settlement in Nicaragua, is established. **1524**		
Nicaragua becomes part of the Federal Republic of Central America. **1823**	**1776**	The U.S. Declaration of Independence is signed.
Nicaragua becomes completely independent. **1838**	**1789**	The French Revolution begins.
American William Walker declares himself king of Nicaragua. **1855**	**1865**	The American Civil War ends.

NICARAGUAN HISTORY

Nicaragua experiences relative stability under conservative governments.	**1860s–1890s**
General José Santos Zelaya takes power.	**1893**
Zelaya reclaims territories along the Atlantic coast that had been occupied by the British.	**1894**
The United States sends military forces to Nicaragua; Zelaya leaves Nicaragua.	**1909**
Forces led by Augusto César Sandino begin a campaign against the U.S. military presence in Nicaragua.	**1927**
Sandino is assassinated.	**1934**
General Anastasio Somoza becomes president following a corrupt election.	**1937**
Anastasio Somoza is assassinated and his son Luis Somoza takes over.	**1956**
The Sandinista National Liberation Front is founded.	**1961**
Luis Somoza dies and is succeeded his brother, Anastasio Somoza Jr.	**1967**
An earthquake devastates Managua.	**1972**
The Sandinistas take control of the government.	**1979**
Rebels called the Contras, with the support of the United States, fight the Sandinistas.	**1980s**
Sandinista leader Daniel Ortega is elected president.	**1984**
Violeta Chamorro becomes the first woman elected president in any Latin American nation.	**1990**
Hurricane Mitch kills four thousand people in Nicaragua.	**1998**
Daniel Ortega is elected president once again.	**2006**
Ortega is reelected in a landslide victory.	**2011**

WORLD HISTORY

1879	The first practical lightbulb is invented.
1914	World War I begins.
1917	The Bolshevik Revolution brings communism to Russia.
1929	A worldwide economic depression begins.
1939	World War II begins.
1945	World War II ends.
1969	Humans land on the Moon.
1975	The Vietnam War ends.
1989	The Berlin Wall is torn down as communism crumbles in Eastern Europe.
1991	The Soviet Union breaks into separate states.
2001	Terrorists attack the World Trade Center in New York City and the Pentagon near Washington, D.C.
2004	A tsunami in the Indian Ocean destroys coastlines in Africa, India, and Southeast Asia.
2008	The United States elects its first African American president.

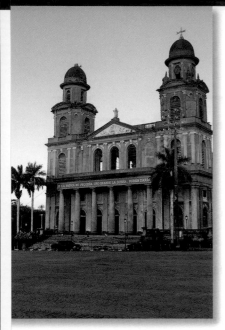

Old Cathedral, Managua

Currency

National population (2015 est.): 6,082,000

Population of largest cities (2016 est.):

Managua	973,087
León	144,538
Masaya	130,113
Tipitapa	127,153
Chinandega	126,387

Landmarks:
- ▶ *Big Corn Island*, Caribbean Sea
- ▶ *Cathedral of León*, León
- ▶ *Momotombo volcano*, Lake Managua
- ▶ *National Museum*, Managua
- ▶ *Old Cathedral*, Managua

Economy: Services make up about half of Nicaragua's economy, with tourism being a growing part of the service sector. Major crops grown for export include sugarcane, coffee, and cotton. Nicaragua also grows a lot of corn, beans, rice, fruits, and vegetables. Nicaraguan factories produce textiles, shoes, chemical products, and food products. Gold and silver are mined in Nicaragua.

Currency: The córdoba. In 2016, 1 córdoba equaled 3 U.S. cents, and US$1.00 equaled 29 córdobas.

System of weights and measures: Metric system

Literacy rate (2015 est.): 83%

Schoolchildren

Dennis Martínez

Common Spanish words and phrases:

Sí	Yes
No	No
Hola	Hello
Adios	Good-bye
Buenas noches	Good night
Buenos días	Good morning

Prominent Nicaraguans:

Gioconda Belli (1948–)
Novelist and poet

Ernesto Cardenal (1925–)
Priest and poet

Violeta Chamorro (1929–)
President

Rubén Darío (1867–1916)
Poet

Asilia Guillén (1887–1964)
Artist

Dennis Martínez (1955–)
Baseball player

Daniel Ortega (1945–)
President and Sandinista leader

Augusto César Sandino (1895–1934)
*Revolutionary leader and inspiration
for the Sandinista movement*

Photo Credits